SCIENCE

THE SCIENCE OF
HOCKEY

RYAN NAGELHOUT

PowerKiDS
press

New York

Published in 2016 by The Rosen Publishing Group, Inc.
29 East 21st Street, New York, NY 10010

First Edition

Editor: Katie Kawa
Book Design: Katelyn Heinle

Library of Congress Cataloging-in-Publication Data

Nagelhout, Ryan, author.
 The science of hockey / Ryan Nagelhout.
    pages cm. — (Sports science)
 ISBN 978-1-4994-1070-9 (pbk.)
 ISBN 978-1-4994-1107-2 (6 pack)
 ISBN 978-1-4994-1143-0 (library binding)
1. Hockey—Juvenile literature. 2. Hockey—Equipment and supplies—Juvenile literature. 3. Sports sciences—Juvenile literature. I. Title.
 GV847.25.N345 2016
 796.962—dc23
                                    2015014984

Manufactured in the United States of America

CPSIA Compliance Information: Batch #WS15PK: For Further Information contact Rosen Publishing, New York, New York at 1-800-237-9932

CONTENTS

Hockey is a fast game full of huge hits, big saves, and amazing goals. Some hockey players can shoot the puck so it travels more than 100 miles (161 km) per hour—a scary thought if it's your job to stop it!

Hockey is different from other sports because it features players with sharp blades on their feet zipping around on a sheet of ice. You need to be tough to play hockey. You also need to be smart. Examples of science are everywhere in a hockey game—from the way the puck moves to the equipment, or gear, used to play the game. Knowing the science behind the sport can help you play better and also stay safe.

Physics is one branch of science you can see in action in a hockey game. Physics is the science of energy and how it interacts with matter.

KINDS OF HOCKEY

HOCKEY CAN BE PLAYED ON MANY DIFFERENT SURFACES, INCLUDING GRASS AND CONCRETE. HOWEVER, ICE HOCKEY IS THE MOST FAMOUS VERSION OF THE SPORT. IN NORTH AMERICA, THE BEST ICE HOCKEY PLAYERS CAN BE FOUND IN THE NATIONAL HOCKEY LEAGUE (NHL). THIS **PROFESSIONAL** LEAGUE INCLUDES TEAMS FROM BOTH THE UNITED STATES AND CANADA, AS WELL AS PLAYERS FROM ALL OVER THE WORLD.

The first thing you need to play hockey is a pair of ice skates. Hockey skates are like boots with big, sharp blades attached to the bottom. Professional hockey players can move around the ice very quickly on their skates.

Hockey players often skate from one end of the rink to the other in order to score a goal or stop the other team from scoring. When they do this, they show velocity. Velocity is the rate at which an object changes its position, which is what players do as they move down the ice.

Hockey players turn their feet and use the inside edge of each skate to cut into the ice in order to slow down or stop. Velocity is important, but so is stopping!

MOVE IT!

WHEN A HOCKEY PLAYER IS SKATING, THEY'RE SHOWING MOMENTUM, WHICH IS MASS IN MOTION. IF YOU'RE MOVING, YOU HAVE MOMENTUM. YOU CAN USE MATH TO FIGURE OUT THE MOMENTUM OF AN OBJECT OR PERSON. MULTIPLY THEIR MASS BY THEIR VELOCITY. HOCKEY PLAYERS OFTEN HAVE MORE MOMENTUM THAN OTHER ATHLETES BECAUSE THEIR SKATES ALLOW THEM TO MOVE AT A HIGHER VELOCITY THAN ATHLETES WHO ONLY MOVE BY RUNNING.

EXTRA POINT

Different skaters need different skates. For example, speed skaters have different skates than hockey players. A speed skater's blades are flat and longer than the boot they sit under.

SPEED SKATER

When a hockey player increases their velocity as they move across the ice, they're said to be accelerating.

Without a stick, a hockey player is just a skater. Early hockey sticks were made of wood. Today, most players use composite sticks, which are sticks made from many different **materials**. Most are made from long strands of graphite, which is a form of **carbon**. The graphite strands are pressed together to make the stick strong but still able to flex, or bend. Fiberglass, which is made of very fine threads of glass, is also commonly used to make composite sticks.

Some sticks are made of two pieces, with a blade and shaft that are glued together. Others are one piece. A hockey stick's shaft can be as long as 63 inches (160 cm), according to the official NHL rule book.

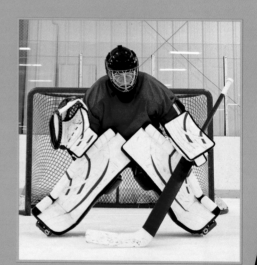

EXTRA POINT

The sticks goaltenders, or goalies, use to stop pucks are different from the sticks used by other players. They're very wide and flat on the bottom. This shape helps them block more of the net when the other team is trying to score.

MASS MATTERS

COMPOSITE STICKS ARE POPULAR BECAUSE THEY'RE STRONG, BUT STILL LIGHTER THAN OTHER KINDS OF HOCKEY STICKS. THE MORE MASS AN OBJECT HAS, THE MORE ENERGY IT TAKES TO MOVE IT. HOCKEY PLAYERS NEED TO BE ABLE TO MOVE THEIR STICK QUICKLY AND EASILY, SO THEY OFTEN LOOK FOR A STICK THAT HAS AS LITTLE MASS AS POSSIBLE WITHOUT BEING EASILY BROKEN.

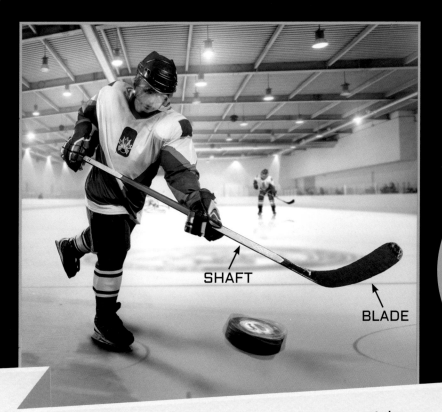

SHAFT

BLADE

New technology has helped make hockey sticks lighter and more flexible than they were in the past.

A hockey stick's flexibility, or flex, is the key to taking big shots. Flex measures how much a stick will bend when a force is applied to it. A force is a push or pull on an object.

The slap shot is the fastest and hardest shot in hockey. Players wind up and shoot the puck as hard as they can, using a motion similar to a golf swing. When taking a slap shot, a hockey player should hit the ice with their stick before they hit the puck. This makes the stick bend, or flex, and allows energy to build up in the stick. When the stick unbends, this stored energy pushes the puck with a greater amount of force than any other kind of shot.

POTENTIAL AND KINETIC ENERGY

A HOCKEY PLAYER CHANGES POTENTIAL ENERGY INTO KINETIC ENERGY WHEN THEY SHOOT THE PUCK. POTENTIAL ENERGY IS STORED ENERGY, SUCH AS THE ENERGY IN A HOCKEY STICK BEFORE IT'S SWUNG. KINETIC ENERGY IS ENERGY USED TO DO WORK. A STICK HAS KINETIC ENERGY WHEN A PLAYER USES IT TO TAKE A SLAP SHOT AND PUSH THE PUCK INTO THE NET.

EXTRA POINT

A tiny crack or chip in a hockey stick can cause it to break when it's flexed or hit by another player's stick. Even a small mistake when making a stick can cause it to break without warning.

Applied force is a push or pull one object **exerts** on another. A hockey player shooting the puck with their stick is an example of applied force.

RUBBER RULES

During skills contests, hockey players sometimes compete to see who has the hardest slap shot. The hardest shot ever measured was taken by Jared Cowen of the Ottawa Senators, who sent a puck flying at 110 miles (177 km) per hour during a team competition in 2014.

There was one problem, though. Cowen didn't use a real puck! A standard NHL puck is made of vulcanized rubber. It measures 1 inch (2.5 cm) thick, 3 inches (7.6 cm) across, and 5.5 to 6 ounces (156 to 170 g) in weight. Someone switched out an official NHL puck for one made of foam, which is much lighter than a rubber hockey puck. The foam puck traveled through the air much faster than a real puck would.

The rubber used to make hockey pucks is rubber that's treated with **chemicals** at a high temperature in order to make it stronger. This process is called vulcanization.

LIGHTER AND FASTER

WHY DID A FOAM PUCK GO FASTER THAN A REAL ONE? THE LESS MASS THE PUCK HAS, THE FASTER IT WILL MOVE OFF A FLEXED STICK'S BLADE. IT TAKES LESS FORCE TO MAKE A FOAM PUCK MOVE THAN A RUBBER PUCK. IF A HOCKEY PLAYER HITS A FOAM PUCK WITH THE SAME AMOUNT OF FORCE THEY USE TO HIT A RUBBER PUCK, THE FOAM PUCK WILL MOVE FASTER.

EXTRA POINT

In 2012, Zdeno Chara set the official NHL record for the fastest slap shot. His record-setting shot made the puck travel 108.8 miles (175 km) per hour.

ON THE CURVE

Today's hockey sticks are curved to the left or right depending on how a player holds their stick. Players can get sticks made to fit whatever style they want as long as it follows NHL rules. The league says stick blades can't curve more than 0.75 inch (19 mm) from a blade's heel to toe.

Why curve a stick's blade in the first place? Curved blades don't make shots faster. Rather, they give a player more control over the puck. It's easier to lift a puck off the ice with a curved stick. A curve also gives a puck more spin when it's shot. This makes the puck more stable while it's moving. Having more stability helps a puck land flat on the ice when it's passed between players.

STAYING STABLE

A QUICKLY SPINNING PUCK IS STABLE BECAUSE IT KEEPS ITS ORIENTATION, OR POSITION, IN THE AIR. IT ALSO EXPERIENCES LESS DRAG, OR AIR RESISTANCE, WHEN SPINNING. AIR RESISTANCE SLOWS THE MOVEMENT OF AN OBJECT, SUCH AS A PUCK, AS IT MOVES THROUGH THE AIR.

EXTRA POINT

When a puck is shot in a way that makes it spin, it becomes a kind of gyroscope. A gyroscope is a spinning disc that can tilt in any direction without falling as it spins.

The curve of a stick's blade is important for creating good passing plays during a hockey game.

FRICTION FORCE

Hockey players often put tape on the blade of their stick. The tape helps them control the puck more easily. It does this by creating friction between the puck and the stick. Friction is a force exerted when an object tries to move across a surface. Generally, friction works to slow the movement of that object. A puck can sometimes move so quickly that it slides right off a player's stick. By creating friction, a player can slow the puck's movement enough to control it.

EXTRA POINT

Friction also exists between a hockey player's skate blades and the ice. Hockey players have the blades sharpened in order to create as little friction as possible. The less friction there is between the blade and the ice, the faster the player will be able to skate.

WORKING WITH WAX

MANY HOCKEY PLAYERS PUT WAX OVER THE TAPE ON THEIR STICK'S BLADE. THE WAX IS WATER-RESISTANT, WHICH MEANS IT KEEPS SNOW OR WATER FROM BUILDING UP ON THE BLADE. THE WAX ALSO CREATES EVEN MORE FRICTION TO HELP PLAYERS CONTROL THE PUCK. THE WAX IS STICKY, SO IT WORKS TO SLOW THE PUCK'S MOVEMENT.

Players also put tape on the shaft of their stick. The tape helps increase the friction between their hands and the stick. This makes the stick easier to hold on to during the game because it won't easily slide out of their hands.

Successful passes in a hockey game are sometimes described as "tape to tape" passes because of the tape on the blades of hockey sticks.

When two hockey players skate toward one another at high speeds, collisions can occur. Collisions happen when one object is pushed into another. How these objects **react** when they come together helps us explain different types of collisions.

An elastic collision occurs when no kinetic energy is lost after two objects come together. No large impacts are perfectly elastic because small amounts of kinetic energy change into other forms of energy whenever two objects collide.

Inelastic collisions occur when kinetic energy changes into a different kind of energy, such as sound or heat. For example, when two hockey players collide, some of their kinetic energy is changed to sound energy. That's how we're able to hear big hits at a hockey game.

Hockey players wear pads to limit injuries. Pads absorb some kinetic energy during collisions.

SAFETY EQUIPMENT, SUCH AS SHOULDER PADS, ELBOW PADS, AND HELMETS, IS MADE OF PLASTIC. THE PLASTIC HELPS **ABSORB** SOME ENERGY FROM HARD HITS AND **DISTRIBUTE** THE FORCE OVER A WIDER AREA OF THE BODY. THIS HELPS HOCKEY PLAYERS PREVENT CERTAIN **INJURIES**, WHICH IS WHY WEARING SAFETY EQUIPMENT IS SO IMPORTANT.

EXTRA POINT

When two hockey players collide, the force of the collision is sometimes strong enough to cause injuries. A concussion is a serious brain injury that can happen due to collisions in hockey, such as two players colliding or a player's head colliding with the boards around the rink.

Goaltenders wear the most equipment because pucks are constantly getting shot their way. Even with all that padding, stopping a slap shot can hurt! Goaltenders wear much bigger chest protectors than other hockey players. They also wear special gloves on each hand. The hand they hold their stick with also uses a blocker, which has a hard, flat surface to stop the puck's motion. A goaltender wears a glove similar to a baseball glove on their other hand. The glove is used to catch the puck.

Goalie pads need to be flexible to allow the player a wide range of motion while still keeping them safe. Soft foam is used to help absorb the force of the puck. Water-resistant leather or plastic keeps the pads from getting wet and heavier because of the ice.

MAKING THE MASK

GOALTENDERS WEAR A MASK TO KEEP THEIR FACE SAFE FROM PUCKS AND STICKS. GOALIE MASKS ARE OFTEN MADE OF FIBERGLASS AND KEVLAR, WHICH IS THE SAME MATERIAL USED TO MAKE BULLETPROOF VESTS. THESE MATERIALS ARE LIGHT ENOUGH TO ALLOW FOR EASY MOVEMENT, BUT STILL STRONG ENOUGH TO PREVENT INJURIES.

EXTRA POINT

A goaltender's job is to stop the puck as it follows its trajectory to the net. A trajectory is the path an object takes in the air.

NHL goaltenders wear about 50 pounds (23 kg) of equipment during each game.

NICE ICE!

The ice is one of the most important parts of any hockey game. A very specific kind of ice is needed for a professional hockey rink. Professional hockey players skate many miles back and forth on the ice during each game. A hockey rink's engineers need to make ice that's strong enough to withstand 20 minutes of hard skating by big, strong players before it can be **resurfaced**.

EXTRA POINT

Concrete is a strong building material made from a mixture of cement, sand, broken rocks, and water.

FROM WATER TO ICE

UNDERSTANDING STATES OF MATTER IS AS IMPORTANT FOR HOCKEY RINK ENGINEERS AS IT IS FOR STUDENTS IN SCIENCE CLASS. CHANGING WATER INTO ICE MEANS CHANGING A LIQUID INTO A SOLID. THIS HAPPENS BY DECREASING ITS TEMPERATURE. IF THE ICE GETS TOO WARM, IT WILL CHANGE FROM A SOLID INTO A LIQUID, WHICH MEANS IT WILL TURN INTO WATER.

An ice surface starts with a big slab of concrete. Under this concrete, miles of pipes are used to quickly freeze water into ice. The ice is made by spraying a thin layer of water onto the concrete and freezing it as little as 0.03125 inch (0.0794 cm) at a time.

STAPLES CENTER, LOS ANGELES

A standard NHL ice rink is an oval that's 200 feet (61 m) long and 85 feet (26 m) wide.

The first layer of ice put down is called a bond. The water needs to freeze quickly to keep from getting dirty. It's filtered many times to remove **excess** oxygen and minerals before it's sprayed to make ice. These impurities make the ice weaker. Too much oxygen or too many minerals in the water can cause skate blades to sink into the ice because it's too soft. Ice makers want clean, clear ice that stays strong over long periods of use.

Ice makers then continue to put down layers of ice so they freeze on top of each other. These special engineers usually build their ice layers to a thickness of about 1 inch (2.5 cm).

During the NHL playoffs—when games can go into overtime and be much longer than they usually are—many ice makers build their ice to about 1.5 inches (3.8 cm) thick. This helps the ice stay strong and last through long games.

EXTRA POINT
Too much oxygen in water is what causes ice cubes to be cloudy instead of clear.

KEEP IT COOL

THE WATER THAT FLOWS THROUGH THE PIPES UNDER THE SLAB OF CONCRETE AT AN ICE RINK IS SALT WATER. THIS KIND OF SALT WATER IS ALSO CALLED "BRINEWATER." WHY IS THE KIND OF WATER IMPORTANT? SALT WATER ACTUALLY HAS A LOWER FREEZING TEMPERATURE THAN WATER WITHOUT SALT. THIS ALLOWS THE WATER TO BE COLD ENOUGH TO KEEP THE CONCRETE CHILLED WITHOUT FREEZING IN THE PIPES.

The chilled salt water that runs through pipes underneath the ice keeps the ice frozen. However, the top of the ice surface constantly changes as players' skates dig into it. Many machines help keep an ice surface in good shape. An ice resurfacer, which is made by companies such as Zamboni or Olympia, actually shaves off the top layer of ice and replaces it with a new one.

Ice resurfacers have a sharp blade that cuts a thin layer of ice into shavings. The shavings are collected in a bin while the ice surface is cleaned. Hot water is then shot out the back of the machine. This water freezes to make a new, smooth sheet of ice.

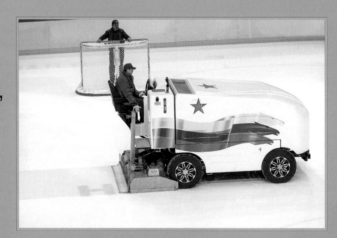

Ice resurfacers are an important piece of technology used during every hockey game.

DOUBLE DUTY

THE ICE AT NHL GAMES IS RESURFACED BETWEEN PERIODS. NHL RINKS USE TWO ICE RESURFACERS AT ONCE, WHICH ALLOWS BOTH MACHINES TO MOVE SLOWLY WHILE THE JOB STILL GETS DONE QUICKLY. RESURFACING THE ICE SLOWLY HELPS IT SET MORE CONSISTENTLY AND NOT BREAK DOWN AS QUICKLY.

THE ICE RESURFACING PROCESS

1 The blade shaves a thin layer of ice from the surface.

2 The shavings are collected and pushed into a snow tank inside the ice resurfacer.

3 Water from the wash-water tank is sprayed onto the ice to rinse away dirt.

4 Dirty water on the ice surface is pushed away and sucked into the ice resurfacer.

5 Clean water from the ice-making tank is spread evenly over the ice surface, filling any holes or cuts in the ice before it freezes.

EXTRA POINT

The top speed of most ice resurfacers is between 9 and 10 miles (14.5 and 16 km) per hour.

An ice surface's biggest enemy is the heat and humidity inside an arena. When an empty arena fills with more than 20,000 people, the climate inside changes and affects the ice. Most buildings try to stay between 50 and 60 degrees Fahrenheit (10 and 16 degrees Celsius).

Humidity is the amount of water vapor in the air. Arenas have big systems to balance humidity because it can affect the quality of ice. If there's too little humidity, the ice can become **brittle**. Too much humidity allows moisture with impurities to sit on the ice. Modern NHL arenas are climate controlled, and arena conditions are constantly monitored. Huge machines are used to pump outside air into the rink as needed.

Engineers work hard to create the perfect playing and viewing conditions for hockey games.

THE FOG GAME

ONE OF THE MOST FAMOUS GAMES IN NHL HISTORY HAPPENED DURING THE 1975 STANLEY CUP FINALS—THE NHL'S MOST IMPORTANT SET OF GAMES—BETWEEN THE BUFFALO SABRES AND THE PHILADELPHIA FLYERS. WITH NO AIR CONDITIONING IN BUFFALO'S MEMORIAL AUDITORIUM, IT WAS SO HOT THAT DENSE FOG FILLED THE RINK. THE GAME HAD TO BE STOPPED A NUMBER OF TIMES BECAUSE PLAYERS COULDN'T SEE THE PUCK!

EXTRA POINT

Fog is created when warm air moves over a cooler surface and condenses, forming a kind of cloud made of water droplets. Fog can appear in a hockey arena if the air is too warm.

Science is always at work when hockey players take the ice. Even the crystal-clear ice they skate on takes lots of engineering to be ready for action. The more you study hockey, the more you'll see it's a game of math and physics, too. The forces behind skating, passing, and shooting all work together to create the big hits, crazy goals, and wild bounces that make an NHL game so exciting.

Try to use what you've learned here the next time you take the ice with your friends. You might be surprised by the way a bit of quick thinking can help you become a hockey superstar!

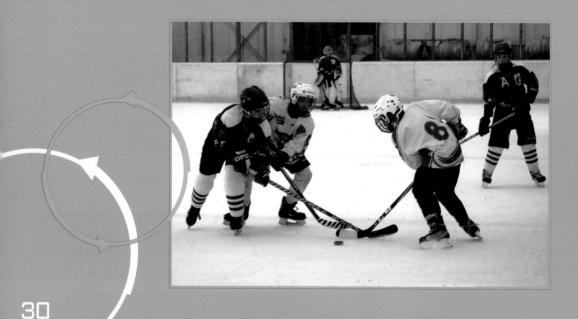

absorb: To take in or soak up.

brittle: Easily broken when stressed.

carbon: A basic substance found in all plants and animals that forms diamonds and coal, among other things.

chemical: Matter that can be mixed with other matter to cause changes.

distribute: To spread out.

excess: An amount of something that is more than what is necessary or desirable.

exert: To put forth.

injury: Harm done to a person's body.

material: Something from which something else can be made.

professional: Having to do with the job someone does for a living.

react: To change or act in response to something.

resurface: To provide a new or fresh top layer.

INDEX

A
accelerating, 7
applied force, 11

B
bond, 24

C
collisions, 18, 19

D
drag, 14

E
elastic collision, 18
equipment, 4, 19,
    20, 21

F
fiberglass, 8, 20
flex, 8, 10, 11, 13
force, 10, 13, 16,
    19, 20, 30
friction, 16, 17

G
goaltenders, 8, 20, 21
graphite, 8

I
ice resurfacer, 26, 27
ice skates, 6, 7, 16,
    24, 26
inelastic collisions, 18

K
kinetic energy, 10, 18

M
mass, 6, 9, 13
momentum, 6

N
NHL, 5, 8, 12, 13, 14,
    21, 23, 24, 27,
    28, 29, 30

P
potential energy, 10
puck, 4, 8, 10, 11, 12,
    13, 14, 15, 16,
    20, 21, 29

S
slap shot, 10, 12,
    13, 20
stick, 8, 9, 10, 11, 13,
    14, 15, 16, 17, 20

T
trajectory, 21

V
velocity, 6, 7

WEBSITES

Due to the changing nature of Internet links, PowerKids Press has developed an online list of websites related to the subject of this book. This site is updated regularly. Please use this link to access the list: www.powerkidslinks.com/spsci/hoc